WITH ALL WE ARE:
Mission, purpose and transformation

DONALD EGGLESTON, M.ED, M.DIV

To BRIAN —

For all that you do to
facilitate mission, purpose
and transformation ...

Don Eggleston

With All We Are
Mission, Purpose and Transformation
Don Eggleston, M Ed, M Div
Mission Works Publishing, LLC

Design: Lopez Needleman Graphic Design, Inc., St. Louis, Missouri, 314.647.6308, mail@lopezneedleman.com, www.lopezneedleman.com

Library of Congress Cataloging-in-Publication Data
Library of Congress Control Number: 2017919607
Don Eggleston
With All We Are: Mission, Purpose and Transformation
ISBN: 978-0-9997417-0-2 (paperback)
Library of Congress subject headings:
    1. BUS085000 Business & Economics / Organizational Behavior
    2. OCC019000 Body, Mind & Spirit / Inspiration & Personal Growth
    3. SEL021000 Self-Help / Motivational & Inspirational

2018

January 2018, Mission Works Publishing.

WITH GRATITUDE

To my teachers — Wick, Jim, Jean

To my "Boys" group — Winch, Pepe, Rufus and Tom

To the Franciscan Sisters of Mary

To our precious sons — Tim and Andy

To my wife, Mary Ann — with gratitude, admiration and love. I love you. I always will.

CONTENTS

"I'm a housekeeper at this hospital. Actually, I'm in charge of Infection Control in this part of the hospital. I keep this operating room perfectly clean and safe to do surgery on each of **my** patients."

How did this happen? How did this hospital employee come to see his daily work in such an elevated and compelling way? How did he recognize his **calling** to serve each of his patients with such devotion? His answer: "My supervisor tells me every day that I am the first step in infection control here."

No matter the role filled by a person in an organization — chief financial officer, property manager, teacher's aide, courtesy clerk, minister — it is shortsighted and pessimistic to think that their only motive is to receive an income and to possess an important title.

People want a purpose. They want a role that reflects their soul.

I worked for thirty years in classroom education, social service, leadership development and organizational mission integration.

I worked with many colleagues who demonstrated a sense of calling — like the infection control specialist /housekeeper. These exemplary employees have one quality in common: They feel deeply connected to the mission and values of their organizations.

This connection is not the result of an internal public relations campaign. This alignment occurs in organizations where fidelity to mission is **intentional** and **unrelenting**. This devotion occurs in settings where leaders **believe** the best about people and where they empower their colleagues to connect to something bigger than themselves.

Examine the stories of organizations that create ethics scandals, with the resulting loss of credibility and business. Read their mission statements, if they can be readily found. When you examine why these crises occured, such as in the wealth management field, it is evident that the mission and values were developed in a superficial, tokenistic fashion and there was no mechanism, from employee recruitment and development to internal operating guidelines, to partnership agreements, to strategic planning, that honored a mission.

There was no **intention** and **attention** around mission, vision, purpose and values.

An honorable, inspiring, and enduring organizational mission is owned and treasured by all who work in that organization and who come to it for service.

To fail to be intentional about your mission and values is to **fail**, period. Along the way, you will lose the hearts and the transformational capacity of the people who once belonged to your organization; they will either leave your company, school, corporation, health system or church or, worst of all, they will be physically present but not really "there."

> It is not always the strongest who survive, but those who best **adapt** who survive and thrive.

If you are a business owner, school administrator, health care or social service director, or a minister, have you ever looked at certain members of your organization (like the operating room housekeeper) and wondered how they stay focused and energized, how they avoid burning out and how they stay engaged in their work?

I have a level of curiosity and admiration for individuals like these. After all, it is both rewarding and demanding to work in the fields of service to others. It is also challenging to lead employees, volunteers, physicians, case workers and parishioners in the challenge of committed service.

In counseling, a common phrase is: "When you stress, you regress." When experiencing high, unrelenting levels of stress, we do regress. We go backwards and become overwhelmed by competing priorities, unforeseen challenges, isolation from supportive relationships and organizational conflict.

I prefer to add an additional piece to the "stress-regress" equation: "When you stress, you regress UNLESS..." When under stress in our leadership roles, we do regress UNLESS:

1. We know **who we are** for all of our strengths, limitations and our defining experiences.
2. We know what we **value** and how those values intersect with the organizations we serve.
3. We understand that the process of personal and organizational change can be both **fluid and awkward**. It is critical for us to adapt to expected and unexpected changes. (I have always appreciated the underlying premise of Darwin's "survival of the fittest" theory: It is not always the strongest who survive and thrive, but those that best adapt. The animals who change fur color in season can hide from predators. Animals who migrate survive the hardships of various seasons. This life-preserving adaptation is a key for us and for the organizations we lead.)
4. We cultivate an **inner stillness** that comes from knowing we are more than our work, more than our titles and accomplishments.

From my experience and observation, UNLESS you develop in the areas I just described, you will lack insight and perspective in your leadership role; and you risk losing your vitality, happiness and credibility as a leader.

■ AN AIRPORT STORY: THE FRAMEWORK FOR OUR LEARNING

Several years ago, in celebration of our twenty-fifth wedding anniversary, my wife, Mary Ann, and I traveled to Ireland. She has relatives there, and had often told me of the monasteries, castles, coastline, music and culture and, certainly, the marvelous people of Ireland.

We landed at the Shannon Airport on an October morning in a fog so dense that we saw the runway lights only seconds before our plane touched down. As we began to navigate the passenger safety process, I was randomly selected for increased scrutiny. I was taken aside by a security agent who asked me a series of questions. He then escorted me to a second agent who asked me the same questions; we then visited a third officer and the same inquiry followed. (I later learned that questions of this sort have been asked at border crossings in many European countries for over a century.)

The questions were:
- **Who are you?**
- **Where are you coming from?**
- **Where are you going?**
- **Why are you going there?**

The process of answering these questions transpired in quick fashion. In fact, my wife did not even notice that I had been questioned by the security personnel. My responses to these questions raised no cause for concern and, thus, I was allowed to collect my luggage and to continue our journey.

These four questions have stuck with me ever since that day. What would happen if we asked these questions not only when moving through an airport but also as we traveled through life? What would occur within and among us if we asked these questions in our relationships, workplaces, schools, congregations, and, certainly, in our quiet moments?

THE AIRPORT QUESTIONS

WHO ARE YOU?

WHY ARE YOU GOING THERE?

WHERE ARE YOU COMING FROM?

WHERE ARE YOU GOING?

WHO ARE YOU?	What **defines** me? Who are the people and what are the experiences that influence me? What are the key elements of my decisions and interactions? What are my abiding strengths? What are my challenges?
WHERE ARE YOU COMING FROM?	What is the defining **mission** of the organization I serve? What does it mean to experience my work as a **calling**? How do I match my personal experience and **values** with those of my organization?
WHERE ARE YOU GOING?	How do I lead **change** in my company, school, parish, service agency or hospital in ways that are enduring, credible and energizing?
WHY ARE YOU GOING THERE?	What enlivens me for the journey of service? What values are integral to me, so integral that, without these values, I would be **unrecognizable** to people who know me? How do I integrate vital relationships, prayer and meditation, and ongoing learning into the evolution of my identity? How do I ensure that I live more **mindfully** rather than languishing in unnecessary worry, rumination, self-doubt and disillusionment?

These questions are the basis for the sections of this book. As such, my thoughts, stories and even the sharing of my struggles are organized around these questions.

So, let's begin. Let's consider these questions as individuals who provide leadership in schools, ministries, clinics, companies, and social service agencies.

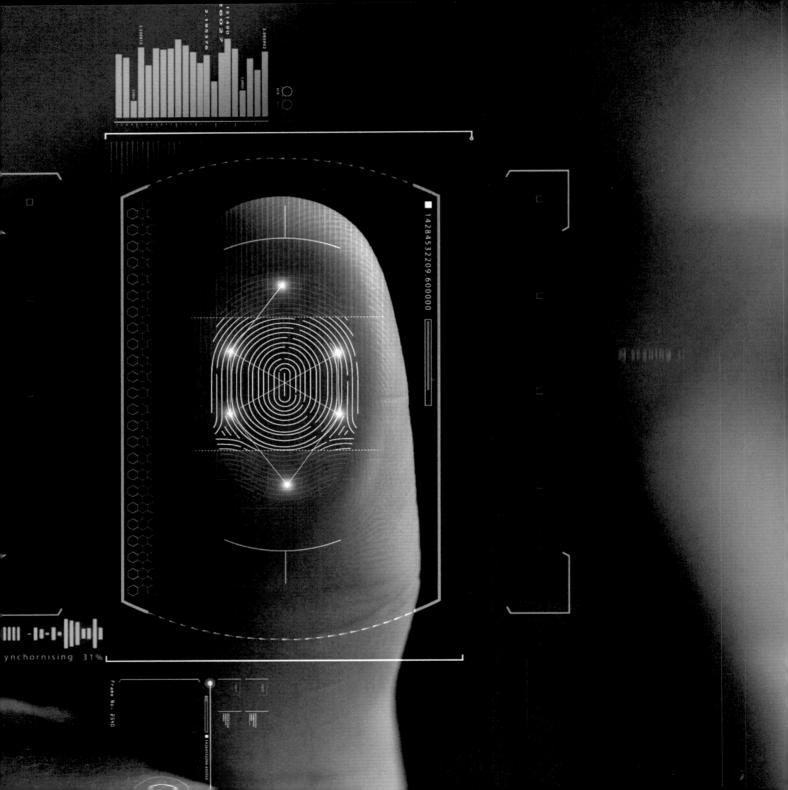

■ "WHO ARE YOU?"

"WHO AM I? REALLY?

I think I know who I am. I administer a school (or hospital or a community service agency or I lead a church).

WHO AM I?

Perhaps you do know who you are, but please consider doing a "re-examination." Perhaps a personal example will help.

I am in my 60s. I was raised in a blue collar family, one of five children. We grew up in an Irish-Catholic neighborhood in St. Louis, Missouri. The daily effects of alcohol abuse in our family had a profound effect on each of us, from fear to disruption to unpredictability to shame to reduced feelings of self-worth. I speak of this to make a point: as adults, we must know who we are deep down inside or we will spin our wheels in both our personal and professional endeavors.

From the hardships of early life, I have learned (and relearned) several tendencies:

- Sometimes I am harshly self-critical, especially when fatigued.
- Sometimes I doubt my abilities, even when there is no evidence to suggest that I do so.
- Sometimes I disregard compliments too readily.
- Sometimes I do these things not because it is good for me, but because it is familiar territory.

- Most times I am a consistently kind and generous person and can easily become overly committed to others' requests.

Knowing where we come from, both limitations and strengths, helps to build interpersonal capacity as well as the ability to be humble and grateful and thereby resilient in the service of others.

I have served in ordained ministry, taught secondary school, and administered social service programs. I spent the greater part of my career in Catholic health care, where I administered community health programs and served as an organizational development consultant. I concluded my professional career as a vice president for mission integration.

I have been married for over thirty years and am the father of two sons. It is a a distinct blessing to be in this family.

Who am I? I am a person who learns, often awkwardly, how important it is to be vulnerable, to seek guidance, to acknowledge loss, to cast aside worry, to regroup, to have enduring purpose, and to be grateful.

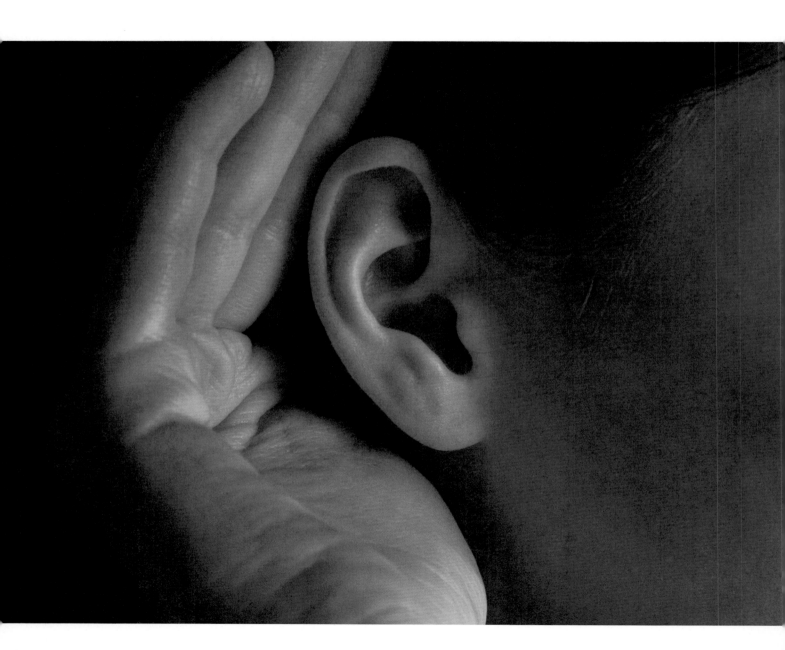

WHOSE VOICE DO YOU HEAR?

The movie **"Dead Poet's Society"** was released in 1989. Early on in the film, English teacher John Keating (played by Robin Williams) enters the life of the new young men who attend Welton Academy, an elite boarding school.

During the orientation to the academic year, the Welton students endured the numbing recitation of course curricula and the accompanying academic expectations. Professor Keating awakens the boys by bringing them to the trophy case in the main entrance and asks them to study the faces of the young men pictured therein: athletes, actors, debate team members and prize students. Keating reminds the students that the young men in the trophy case are now "fertilizing daffodils." He states that the same fate awaits them some day. Keating counters his somber message with the exclamation to "Seize the day, boys! Make your lives extraordinary." The boys are hooked. This class becomes the occasion for soul searching, discovery and adaptation to great loss.

I find it helpful to reflect occasionally on those who are in my personal trophy case. As Professor Keating suggests in his course introduction, these individuals teach you to make your life extraordinary. Recall why they matter to you. Ask yourself if you continue to embody what they taught you.

I mentioned earlier that I grew up in a family that knows the effects of alcohol abuse. While my dad's misuse of alcohol greatly affected his abilities as a father, I was also given many "fathers" along the way:

- My baseball coach, Mr. Messel
- A college professor, Dr. John Wickersham
- A seminary administrator, Father Hugh O'Donnell,
- My uncle, Jim Lopez
- My father-in-law, Ed Harty, and
- My own dad.

They are in my trophy case. They taught me to integrate and overcome.

> STOP AND REFLECT, PLEASE.
> Who teaches you to make your life extraordinary?
> Who is in your trophy case?

ADJUST YOUR LENSES

In the course of my annual vision examination, my optometrist will ask: "Is this lens clearer? Which lens is better?" From her examination and from my response to questions like these, she describes my visual acuity.

The *lenses* through which you see your strengths and limitations can be a real asset to you in your leadership of others. By strengths I do not necessarily mean the ability to plan, organize or develop budgets but your character strengths. Martin Seligman, Ph.D., has led significant research in what he calls "signature strengths." Seligman insists that the utilization of these strengths leads people to **survive** and then to **thrive** in challenging circumstances.

I would recommend a look at Seligman's work — Search online for "Signature Strengths" or "Values in Action Inventory of Strengths." Included among the twenty-four signature strengths are:

- Creativity and Originality
- Spirituality and Sense of Purpose
- Love of Learning
- Perspective/Wisdom
- Social Intelligence
- Teamwork and Loyalty

The intentional use of key signature strengths will have true impact on interactions, decisions and effectiveness.

At the same time, acknowledge limitations — too quick to make decisions, overly sensitive to criticism, threatened by the ideas of others, fear of conflict — so that neither decisions nor credibility are compromised.

For over 10 years, I regularly ask this question of people who reported to me as well as those with whom I served on teams: "What do I do day-to-day that makes your work easier or more difficult to do?" You learn a lot about your strengths and limitations from their responses. The degree to which you listen to the responses can only build greater trust.

As we leave this section, resolve to frequently ask yourself and others the first border crossing question: "WHO AM I?"

ANOTHER RESOURCE that has been enlightening to me is the Enneagram, which is a seasoned inventory. The Enneagram is a resource for identifying tendencies and strengths and it also assists those who utilize it to understand that there is a "shadow" side to our tendencies and motivations. Its spiritual orientation is helpful for those who want to achieve greater clarity through their spiritual "lenses." The Enneagram resources I recommend are Suzanne Stabile and Franciscan priest Father Richard Rohr.

■ "WHERE ARE YOU COMING FROM?"
The Necessity of Your Alignment With an Authentic Organizational Mission

The **authentic** mission of an organization is its **lifeblood.** The mission reflects the reason for the existence of an organization, church or academic institution. The stated mission is what draws people to both serve on behalf of an organization and to come to the same organization for compassionate service.

The mission reflects what you do and **why** you do it — why you teach, why you provide health services, why you are a church community.

Clearly formulated and articulated, the mission is the heart of your decisions and it will **unify** at decisive times.

When deeply embedded, the mission is reflected in every deliberation, decision and encounter.

> Dirty
> deeds
> done
> cheap
> by a guy
> who does
> it right

This handwritten sign was affixed to the side of a truck in rural Wisconsin. A purpose statement, and a resulting promise from this one-person corporation.

Twenty years ago, I was asked to serve as a member of a cross-organizational team with my employer, SSM Health. Our challenge was to establish a new mission and values statement for our organization. My participation in this process became the most profound experience of my career.

In 1997, SSM Health consisted of sixteen hospitals, a home care and hospice division, and multiple support functions (i.e., supply chain, business services, human resources, information technology, etc.). There were twelve thousand employees throughout the organization. Each of the hospitals had its own mission statement and many of the statements were several paragraphs long.

The president of SSM Health at that time, Sister Mary Jean Ryan, FSM, challenged our team to develop a mission statement that was "easily remembered and representative of who we are" as a health system.

Our team embarked on a process that included conducting interviews and focus groups with approximately three thousand employees, physicians and volunteers.

In conducting these interviews, we utilized the principles of Appreciative Inquiry. The intent of Appreciative Inquiry is to identify the *positive core* of an organization, the driving force which holds a group together in its most

The mission reflects not just what you do but **why** you do it — why you teach, why you provide health services, why you are a church community.

difficult times. Among the questions we asked in our interviews with our employees were:

- "What keeps you working on your most difficult day?"
- "What is the important quality required to work with people who are suffering?"
- "Describe the co-workers with whom you most love to work."
- "When we are at our best in this hospital/clinic/office, what does it look like?"
- "Describe what makes you proud to work at SSM Health."
- "Tell me a story about what you think is the heart of SSM."

Out of this process emerged the SSM Mission Statement:

"Through our exceptional health care services, we reveal the healing presence of God."

We also articulated five values:

- **Compassion:** We reach out with openness, kindness and concern.
- **Respect:** We honor the wonder of the human spirit.
- **Excellence:** We expect the best of ourselves and one another.
- **Stewardship:** We use our resources wisely.
- **Community:** We cultivate relationships that inspire us to serve.

The development of the questions, the facilitation of interviews and focus groups, the summary of the responses and the final articulation of the mission and values were all done by staff employees of SSM Health.

What a transformative process!

The mission and values became the foundation for the following:

- The strategic planning process.
- The discernment process for determining future partners in our ministry.
- Significant elements of human resources practices (i.e., employee recruitment, orientation, performance evaluation, performance appraisals and feedback)
- Executive orientation and formation.

I was working as an internal organizational development consultant at the time the mission and values statement was developed, and I often used the mission and values as a guide for managers in holding employees accountable for performance. For example, if an employee was indifferent toward a patient who could not easily speak English, it was a diminishment of our value of community. If an employee was habitually late for work, the value of stewardship was not being fulfilled.

Even today, during employee huddles (i.e., brief employee meetings on shift change in which essential patient and operational information is exchanged), employees devote a few minutes every few days to ask together: "How did we see the values of compassion, respect, excellence, stewardship and community at our center in recent days? How did we serve as a healing presence to our patients and visitors?"

The responses are often simple and affirming of the good that can occur in the course of a work day.

The responses are often simple and affirming of the good that can occur in the course of a work day.

DEEPENING THE VALUES OF A SCHOOL COMMUNITY

St. John Vianney High School is a Catholic, all-boys secondary school in St. Louis. The school is sponsored by The Society of Mary (Marianists), which was founded two hundred years ago in France by Blessed William Joseph Chaminade.

I have served on the board of St. John Vianney High School for eleven years, twice serving as board chairperson.

The Marianist order asks that those who serve in the universities, secondary and elementary schools, embrace and bear witness to the Characteristics of Marianist Education (CMEs) which are:

· Educate for formation in faith
· Provide an integral, quality education
· Educate in the family spirit
· Educate for service, justice and peace
· Educate for adaptation and change

These characteristics serve as the framework for strategic planning, for academic innovation, for school counseling services, for developmental and disciplinary practices and for evaluation of the overall effectiveness of the school.

At the St. John Vianney board meetings, the characteristics of Marianist Education are printed on the meeting agenda. At the conclusion of the meeting, we review our deliberations and ask which of the CMEs were evident in our discussion and decisions.

We regularly invite Vianney students to the meeting to share with us what they have learned from his involvement in service projects, theatre, athletics, student council, academics and other pursuits. Without being asked, the students often couch their remarks in the context of the CMEs.

The school administration, faculty and students also complete an annual assessment of the activities of the school which reinforce the CMEs, from academics to co-curriculars to faculty development to campus symbols and signage.

It is this focused, intentional process that enables the school to remain faithful to what we value.

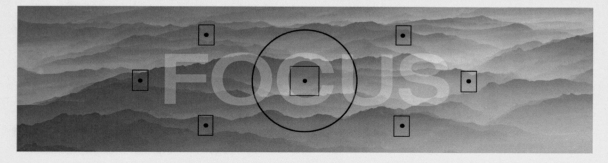

YOUR ORGANIZATION'S MISSION: CULTIVATING AN INHERITANCE

When my father was dying, he elected to give his children and grandchildren personal possessions by which we would remember him. Some received the tools from his workroom, some received family pictures; the younger grandchildren received piggy banks loaded to the top with quarters. I received my dad's shaving brush and mug and his shoeshine kit. I placed the brush and mug on top of the mirror in the bathroom. Every time I shine my shoes, I think of my dad.

You may have received an inheritance yourself, perhaps something with more worldly value, like money, securities or property. As with any inheritance, the challenge is to use it wisely and not to squander it.

SSM Health's History

In 1872, Mother Mary Odilia Berger arrived in St. Louis from Germany along with four companion sisters, and responded to victims of a smallpox epidemic devastating the community. Such was their devotion that they initially became known as the "smallpox sisters." The spirit of our founding sisters and those who followed after them has taken hold in multiple states, several foreign countries and in the hearts of those who have benefited from their health care and social service ministries.

As her death approached in 1880, Mother Odilia encouraged the sisters in her fledgling congregation to "continue courageously for the love of God." In speaking these words, which are referenced to this day throughout SSM Health, Mother Odilia leaves an inheritance, a pearl of great price.

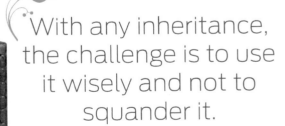

With any inheritance, the challenge is to use it wisely and not to squander it.

> Keeping in mind Mother Odilia's encouragement to "continue courageously," I offer one of the richest meanings of the word, which is rooted in "cor" (Latin for "heart"): "To tell the story of your life with your whole heart."

More than 100 years later, at a leadership conference at SSM Health, Sister Mary Jean Ryan, FSM, then president of the organization, spoke for her congregation when she said to those in attendance, "This ministry is in your hands." Sr. Mary Jean left us an inheritance. Her words, "It's in your hands," are repeated in employee orientations, formation programs, annual Mission Days programs and in countless settings across SSM Health.

Keeping in mind Mother Odilia's encouragement to "continue courageously," I offer one

of the richest meanings of the word, which is rooted in "cor" (Latin for "heart"): "To tell the story of your life with your whole heart."

The Franciscan Sisters of Mary told the story of their collective lives by feeding the hungry, nursing the sick, advocating for both human dignity and an abiding love for the earth. This is the inheritance that they have blessed SSM Health employees with for the past 145 years.

Cultivating Our Inheritance

How do we cultivate an inheritance of this magnitude? Let's begin with a deeper understanding of cultivation. Several years ago, I was asked to facilitate the SSM Mission Days program in Wisconsin. This was an important endeavor, as we had recently acquired another organization and were working to integrate our two cultures. My topic was *Cultivating Community*. While preparing, I took a personal trip to visit people I know in Illinois and Kentucky who raise both crops and thoroughbred horses. I asked many questions about cultivation, and here is what I learned:

1. When you work in the earth and with animals, you soon learn *what things are in your control.*

"I have lost crops in the past three years to both drought and flood," said one farmer. These disasters occurred despite his access to satellite technology and National Weather Service information. The farmer told me that he learned about "soil recovery, personal resilience, faith in God, and the power of prayer" from these experiences. What is in your control? What is truly possible? What will you influence as a leader? Give thought to this.

2. You learn how to nourish and nurture soil, animals, water sources and even co-workers. "You nurture the crops with the big picture in mind," said the southern Illinois farmer.

   Over the years, I learned that organizations sometimes overlook the need to nourish and nurture employees in their haste to bring about change and new structures. On an individual level, for example, an applicant certainly might accept a job because it provides an income. The same applicant might be accepted for the position because of his or her existing credentials (i.e., advanced degree, certifications, etc.). These two motives alone will not sustain when the inevitable tough stretches occur in a field like health care, such as patient deaths, steep learning curves or conflicts with colleagues. Without deep purpose, an employee is likely to default to statements like, "They don't pay me enough for this nonsense," or "I can't believe I went to school for this!" In this instance, what is lacking is the nurturing of a sense of calling, a consistent sense that my work matches my soul. The theologian Frederick Buechner speaks of this calling as "the place where your deep

gladness and the world's deep hunger meet." Arrival at this place requires nurturing of all involved in the organization's mission.

The nurturing process begins with the employee recruitment and selection process. Begin with building your employee candidate interview questions from your organizational values. For example: "Would

We all need work that reflects our very souls.

you describe the mission and values of a place where you worked previously and how you demonstrated that mission and those values in your daily work."

In terms of performance management, give all developmental feedback in light of your organization's mission and values. For example: "The way that you guided our new employee reflects our value of community." Or, "Your sarcastic comments about our customer/clients pulls away from our value of respect. This is not who we are and I will not allow it to continue."

Be sure to build into organizational job descriptions the behaviors that reflect values

and hold employees as accountable for those behaviors as you do for the completion of their job duties.

Commend individuals and teams for improvement. **Celebrate success** and progress. Nurture the "soil" in which people labor.

3. One farmer told me about an age-old practice that still has relevance in his farming: allowing a field to lie fallow. He described it as "purposeful waiting." He educated me on how you cannot use a field relentlessly without giving it necessary time to recover; he told me that you move a field to a fallow state by reason of "facts and instinct." Perhaps when we work within our organizations, we might look for what is absolutely crucial in terms of strategic, operational and mission integration and what is best left to "purposeful waiting."

   For example: Do you really think it is beneficial to have emails, texts, and attachments being sent at all hours of the day? At what point do organizations look at the potentially destructive effects of this practice?

4. My favorite: "Fertilizer is key, the natural stuff," said my pal who raises thoroughbreds. "On this horse farm, do you know where I get the good stuff to grow those whopper tomatoes? You ought to be around here on a hot summer day in Kentucky!" He proceeded to show me a vehicle called a "honey wagon" that tumbles horse manure and water in such a way that it can be spread on the field where he grows several kinds of vegetables.

What do we learn from "fertilizer" when it appears in our organization? Do we have the humility (from the Latin word "humus," or "soil") to learn from previous attempts at organizational change or integration that did not go so well? On an immediate level, what steps do we take to integrate new people into a work group? What can be done to learn from conflicts in a work setting? In essence, what can we learn from the honey wagon when it rolls through town?

For any organization to successfully cultivate and integrate an inheritance, it requires an intentional, deliberative approach to be authentic to its history and heroic figures. We must be fully aware of how our organization can begin "to tell the story of our lives" with full individual and collective hearts. This process fosters the necessary courage for the actual integration to follow.

SSM Health developed an extensive assessment methodology for evaluating the potential of mission integration. During the due diligence process, prior to determining the strategic and operational compatibility of potential partners, an extensive evaluation is conducted as it relates to their history, mission and ethics, as well as their understanding of health care as a ministry of the Catholic Church. This discernment process lead to decisions both to undertake and dismiss new partnership opportunities.

Look To One Another

While organizational culture is certainly complex, it is forged by identifying what everyone has in common — the collective desire to be identified by more than job duties, roles and professional credentials. We all desire work that reflects our very souls.

When new people to your organization through acquisitions or mergers, one simple question that yields a lot of information with employee groups is this: "Tell me about a part of the culture where you worked before that you would like to be integrated in the new organization." This question has been most beneficial in generating dialogue over the initial phases of integration. Other key questions to ask include:

- "Who are the people emerging as true leaders during this time of change in this organization?"
- "As you understand the mission and values of our organization, where do you see them taking hold?"
- "What is a difficult part of joining this organization?"

From responses to questions like these, you come to see what wants nurturing and what wants to lie fallow.

The cultivation of an organizational inheritance is a process of forming a culture. It is progressively built through interaction upon interaction, question upon question, decision upon decision.

To do anything less would be to squander an inheritance.

Nurture the "soil" in which people labor.

■ "WHERE ARE YOU GOING?"
Leading Change in Lifegiving and Credible Ways

Change occurs in your business, school, health center, agency or church for a variety of reasons:

- The change of an industry **standard** (e.g., accreditation, certification, reduction in availability of grants);
- A desire to set your **institution** apart (e.g.., opportunity to innovate);
- An **unexpected event** (e.g., decline in census membership or enrollment, fewer customers, etc.).

One of your roles as a leader is to lead change in such a way that your organization's mission is vital, relevant and faithful to its spiritual and religious core.

I offer you some thoughts and practices that can be readily applied in leading those involved in the change process. I recommend two authors whose research in change management is thorough and easily adapted. I have seen their ideas work and I want to credit them for their wisdom around leading change, whether change is desired or thrust upon you.

William Bridges, author of *Managing Transactions: Making the Most of Change.* This is a timeless book which describes the stages that are typically experienced by the individuals involved in the change process. His "Ending – Middle – Beginning" Model is priceless.

In explaining his model, Bridges uses the example of telling stories. Whatever the story or fable, we expect a process which includes a beginning (to introduce the story and its characters), a middle (to add depth to the story) and an ending (which often teaches a lesson or moral).

By contrast, Bridges says, change stories have an ending first. What ends might be the way we did our work, the relationships we had, even the core purpose of the organization. Then the middle, where we redefine our purpose, conduct small-scale pilot projects and keep track of snags in the implementation of a change process, set new expectations and point to reasons for hope. When we do our "middle" work as an organization, a new beginning occurs.

Alan Deutschman has written many articles and books. My favorite is *Change or Die: Three Keys to Change at Work and in Life.* Deutschman based his research on the key factors in successful change in three disparate groups:

- Cardiac patients with challenging diagnoses;
- Ex-offenders with a dramatically reduced recidivism (return to prison) rate;
- Formerly underperforming employees (i.e., increased errors and injuries) in an automobile manufacturing plant who functioned at a high level of effectiveness after organizational intervention.

TRANSITION MODEL (Adapted from the work of William Bridges)

ENDING

For some:
Grief
Anger
Anxiety
Disorientation
Self-doubt
Loss of identity

For others:
New challenge
Creativity

MIDDLE/NEUTRAL

For some:
Skepticism
Uncertainty
Decreased motivation
Absenteeism

For others:
Reorientation
Redefinition
Creativity

BEGINNING

For all:
Openness to change
Renewal of commitment
to the group and roles

CREATING LASTING CHANGE (Adapted from the work of Alan Deutschman)

FROM

FEAR
People are emotional.
Overwhelm their emotions
and they will change.

FACTS
People are rational, right?
Give them the facts and
they will change.

FORCE
Threaten or coerce and
they will change.

TO

RELATE
Form relationships which
inspire a sense of hope and
fosters a belief that things
can be better.

REFRAME
Look at your situation as an
opportunity to improve over
where you were previously.

REPEAT
Undertake little actions
daily that help you to
change around what
truly matters.

His **"Relate – Repeat – Reframe"** model for ensuring vital change is required (and groundbreaking) reading for leaders. I thought so much of Alan's work that I recruited him to speak at a leadership conference while I worked at SSM Health.

Essentially, Deutschman states that we often try to bring about change by employing a "fear, facts and force" model to get people to change. He is emphatic that this does not work. Instead, Deutschman found from his research that when people **relate** to the need for change they **reframe** their thinking about the change. Then, they **repeat** the new behaviors frequently enough that the desired change becomes the "new normal."

An example: I met a patient who was waiting to be discharged from a hospital following surgery.

He explained his motives for his enthusiasm:

1. His daughter was being married in eight weeks and he wanted to walk her down the aisle to meet her husband.
2. His wife was buried several years earlier on a hillside in the town cemetery, and he could not reach her grave with "his old hip."

He was not motived by fear, facts or force. He was motivated by what he related to (i.e., his daughter's wedding and visiting his wife's grave) and he reframed his thinking (i.e., going to rehab in order to be a deeper part of his family) so that he could repeat the necessary steps to achieving independence of movement.

> Deutschman found from his research that when people **relate** to the need for the change they **reframe** their thinking about the change. Then, they **repeat** the needed behaviors frequently enough that the desired change becomes the "new normal."

THE CRISIS WHEEL:
A FRAMEWORK FOR LEADING CHANGE IN CRITICAL TIMES

The word *crisis* in its Greek origin translates as "to choose or to decide" — not to "freak out." In a hospital, when a patient becomes critically (which comes from the same root word) ill, the staff does not freak out. Rather, the response team, under the direction of a physician, follows a course of action such as calling a code, beginning emergency intervention, stabilizing of the patient, etc. When a school, hospital, agency or church experiences a crisis, however unsettling, the fact remains that a choice, a course of action must be undertaken.

A friend of mine, Fr. Jim Krings, knew all about crisis. As a priest, Jim served as an associate pastor, high school administrator, hospital chaplain and mission leader. More importantly, for over one-third of his life, Jim survived three bouts with cancer, finally succumbing at the age of sixty-three.

Redrawing The Circle

When Jim became ill with cancer, he told me that the diagnosis of cancer at age forty "just didn't fit." Until his diagnosis, Jim felt that he had a "clearly defined circle" of his life that included being a parish priest, a son, brother, uncle, friend and a St. Louis Cardinals "baseball nut." He realized that he had to *redraw the circle* to include the reality that he now had cancer. Jim did, then, redraw the circle

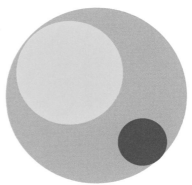

to include going to chemotherapy and radiation treatments, to curtailing some of his ministerial commitments and to spending more time with friends. Eventually, the circle expanded to include volunteering at the Missouri Botanical Garden, adopting several cats (named Pearl, Rabbi, Rani [meaning Princess] and Angel) and changing the focus of his ministry from parish work to health care chaplaincy. Talk about redrawing the circle!

In terms of your leadership roles, consider the necessity of redrawing the circle in your approach and disposition. For instance, if you are in educational leadership, did you ever think you would have to deal with cyberbullying or provide laundry services in your school for students who experience the shame of wearing unlaundered clothing each day? If you are in health care, you know that health care services are often provided in complex socio-economic circumstances or that some patients can be non-compliant when their cooperation is essential for their recovery. Redrawing the circle becomes essential in your leadership role.

Recently, I visited with a priest who had been charged with blending two parishes into one community of faith. He described his frustration with the "turfy" behavior of many parishioners. He told me that he wanted to say to people: "We are the church, right? We are, first and foremost, believers, right?"

I suggested that he ask these questions in a sermon (and probably alienate more than a few parishioners). Better yet, I suggested that he could place in the sanctuary all of the things that people were quibbling over —

- Hymnals
- Stations of the Cross
- Soccer uniforms
- Priest vestments
- Tickets for the homecoming raffle
- The sacred altar vessels

and inform people that these items were keeping them from seeing each other for who they are. The combined parish inventory list was a liability and an impediment to building community, plain and simple.

Last I checked, people come to a church for encouragement, to be consoled when losses occur, to bury their loved ones, to witness their children's marriages, to gain perspective when they are suffering and to be challenged and inspired.

He didn't stuff the sanctuary as I suggested. He did use the idea of redrawing the circle as the foundation for his interactions and preaching.

Creating The Crisis Wheel

As I mentioned earlier, after his second bout with cancer, Father Jim Krings developed a methodology for dealing with crisis. The following model, the *Crisis Wheel*, was derived from the struggle for his health; however, this model certainly applies to achieving organizational health in the midst of change. Jim Krings' Crisis Wheel looks like the drawing below.

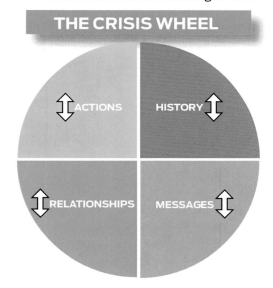

THE CRISIS WHEEL

ACTIONS / HISTORY / RELATIONSHIPS / MESSAGES

Jim used this model to help him through two decades of health challenges. Here's how. When it came to his personal history, what could Jim build upon? He had a favorable history of trusting his physicians and caregivers. He had a positive history of complying with treatment protocols as well as raising questions when necessary. He knew from his experiences as a patient how to read his body — when to rest, when to press on and when to let others help him. He also knew to disregard the negative aspects of his personal history (i.e., the inclination to worry and fear) as much as possible.

In terms of messages, what was beneficial to Jim? Messages like "I can overcome this with help," "God is with me," and "I don't have to get through this gracefully" served him as well. Anything other than this type of internal message needed to be disregarded.

For Jim, relationships were critical during his struggle for good health. In his relationships with his doctors and caregivers, Jim looked for what he called "a mixture of candor and encouragement" in their conversations. On the other hand, Jim minimized contact with individuals who, while well-intentioned, often raised his anxiety in his encounter with them.

Finally, during the times when cancer reappeared, Jim focused on beneficial actions, such as limiting his ministerial commitments, volunteering at the Missouri Botanical Gardens and closely following his beloved St. Louis Cardinals. He steadfastly avoided choices such as over commitment and reading so much about his illness that it caused his anxiety to surge.

Now let's look at the Crisis Wheel as it applies to our organizational leadership roles in times of crisis.

What **history** do we bring to a crisis? What serves us well from that history? Have we previously rallied as an organization in tough

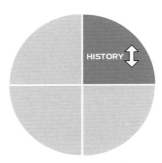

times? Do we have a history of pulling together as a group? Where are these examples of how we have adapted successfully to challenges to our viability? Are there heroes in our past to call upon as examples for us?

What if our organizational history does not serve us well? Is there a history of unresolved conflicts or intense rivalries between departments? Have we had unacknowledged cost reduction strategies (i.e., layoffs) in the recent past?

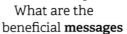

What are the beneficial **messages** to be articulated during a crisis or period of dramatic change? Examples: "What are the compelling reasons for the change and why is there reason for optimism?" "How much do we know about the current status of the change initiative?" Also, don't overwhelm people with information. Ask for their perceptions or concerns — in groups or individually.

Untrue detrimental messages (such as unfounded rumors) need to be identified or minimized.

Who are the key people to have at the forefront of the change — those who are

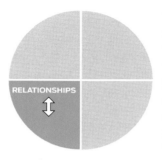

widely respected, insightful, talented, unafraid to speak the truth? Who are internal people who are good at process design and employee communications? Who are the credible people who will appropriately raise issues?

What **relationships** do not serve us well in the change initiative? How do we compassionately and directly address those who project their own anxieties onto the greater group? Who are any parties trying to steamroll or intimidate those with whom they differ? Parties on either side of the change initiative need to be held accountable for any behavior which undermines the situation.

Based upon what we know at each point in a crisis or significant change, what are the most beneficial **actions** or steps? Which actions best align with the mission? (Hint: All the actions should.) Which actions incorporate legitimate

concerns raised by colleagues? What are the key actions you need to take as the leader? Which actions should not be undertaken? Examples: Avoiding opportunities to communicate key messages; violations of confidentiality in the due diligence process.

My buddy, Jim, certainly applied his Crisis Wheel in his personal struggle and even in his palliative care and hospice days. However, he also influenced many of us who worked alongside him in health care. I facilitated the use of the Crisis Wheel when teams were faced with financial downturns, revisions in how we delivered patient care and, most importantly, helping nurses and other caregivers to deal with the grief when patients died.

Crisis: "To choose, to decide." Thank you, Jimmy.

"Somebody has to do something!
It's just incredibly pathetic that it has to be us!"

Jerry Garcia, The Grateful Dead

SIMPLE STEPS TO HELP PEOPLE UNDERTAKE CHANGE: EGGLESTON'S TOP TEN

While it is so crucial in the change process to have a **purpose, plan, budget, goals and measures** and **timeframes**, it is equally important to **communicate** in ways that get the critical mass of people on board. If you are changing the school curriculum, changing how the service is delivered in your clinic, or having to blend two churches, the process of communications with all involved (i.e., both employees and recipients of your services) is essential.

The following is "Eggleston's Top Ten" for enhancing both colleague and end user support for a change initiative. It doesn't come from a book; it comes from my experience and observations.

1 What is the **purpose** of the change? What makes it necessary? How does this change help us to honor and fulfill our mission?

2 What is the **desired result**? What will it look like when the change is successful (i.e., ACT scores will improve, response time to patients will be quicker, younger or more diverse people will join our church, etc.)

3 What are the **key steps** or **milestones** in achieving the plan? (Create a chart or other visual medium; they need to see how progress will be monitored. Use clear, understandable visuals where needed.)

4 What **resources** are needed? Money. Time. People on teams. Training and coaching. IT support. (A note about training and coaching. People can "freeze" if they feel that they lack the skills required for the new world. I have frozen twice in my career and benefited greatly from education and coaching in each instance.)

5 Decide upon **key messages** that give hope. Plan to speak them over and over.
- "We want to do this because _____."
- "We will not stay in the current place because _____."
- "We want to know what the key challenges will be for you. We have anticipated some of them, but please identify for us what skills will be needed in this new structure."
- "What we will control is _____."
- "Here's how each of you can help: _____."
- "How else can you all help (individually or collectively)?"_____
- "At the end of each individual or group conversation, please tell me what you understand to be the key points from our conversation/meeting." Then listen and clarify.

Be awake to transformation in your midst.

6 Emphasize not only **what** change is happening but **why** it is occurring. I observed the *what and why* phenomenon frequently in my health care career. A patient would be told the "whats" of their diagnosis — the diagnostic findings, a recommended course of treatment, etc. However, what was often rattling around inside were the why questions: "Why am I sick?" "Why am I sick now — when I am young or ready to retire?" When you are communicating with people about change, focus on the why as well as the what.

7 Regularly **monitor** and **evaluate** the change process. Determine if any part needs to be revised, delayed or re-established.

8 Recognize that some people may **opt out**. Some people may not be interested in the new state of your organization. Is it better to have them leave the organization (and acknowledge these departures) than it is to have them stick around and mentally leave?

9 Strive for more than change. Seek **transformation**. An image that comes to mind is that of a transformer, which takes all of the wild, potentially dangerous electrical energy and trans-

forms it for safe use. Leaders of change take all of the "wild" energy of hope, aspiration, cynicism, human desire, human fault and transform it for good. Pledge to lead a transformative process that best serves your patients, clients, students, congregation and colleagues.

10 You are a **model of change** for others. Read. Study. Listen to people whose viewpoint differs from yours. Ask for feedback on your performance. Again, ask "What do I do day-to-day that makes your work easier or more difficult to accomplish?"

A final thought for this section: For your own mental health, pay attention to the amazing changes that do occur in your hospitals, clinics, agencies, congregations and schools. Notice and celebrate progress.

Be awake to transformation in your midst. Notice the kids in your school who have changed dramatically for the good or a teacher who is growing into his or her calling to teach. If you are in health care, notice the patients who are restored to health, who are given back their lives.

You are a part of school, service, ministerial and healing communities when circles are redrawn and transformation occurs.

Remain awake to this core, blessed truth.

■ "WHY ARE YOU GOING THERE?"
What Sustains You in Your Journey of Service?

The first three "airport" questions highlight personal identity, mission integration and leading change. The final question "Why are you going there?" acknowledges that caring for ourselves is essential when we lead others in the service of others. Reflect on your mission as a leader — principal, president, pastor, department chair or administrator. How often do the people where you lead line up to ask how YOU are doing during periods of crisis, transition and change?

I have experienced what I call "service exhaustion" on two occasions in my career. The opportunity to serve becomes an opportunity for resentment. Being counted on by others may become an occasion to count how much more I am doing than anyone else.

As my high school Latin teacher would often say to us: "Nemo dat quod non habet." He translated it as "You can't give what you ain't got." Terrible grammar, but you get the idea. It is very easy to fall into levels of exhaustion in our work or ministry if we do not build the emotional, spiritual and relational scaffolding required for leadership responsibilities.

In this final chapter, I offer what I have learned — often the hard way — about caring for self and reaffirming "why you are going there."

1. **Cultivate places for silence, prayer and meditation.** Life as we experience it today is so cluttered with social media, 24-hour news, "business" communications with little respect for personal boundaries, political outrage and way too much reality TV. This is an unrelenting phenomenon and it creates an underlying level of anxiety, distraction and preoccupation that is wrongly considered to be "just a part of life."

While working in health care, I experienced the benefit of applied technology (i.e., diagnostic imaging, virtual consultation, telemedicine). The same could be said for education — distance learning, online courses and consultations with peers. However, the excessive

> As my high school Latin teacher would often say to us: "Nemo dat quod non habet." He translated it as "You can't give what you ain't got."

> As a simple practice,
> I sit quietly for
> 20 minutes a day
> (starting from two
> minutes a day ten
> years ago). I call this
> time "silence without
> a goal."

exposure to technology — just watch families out to dinner at a noisy sports bar all checking their smart phones — will overwhelm, discourage and sedate us. Hence, the desire for quiet and stillness. It's actually acceptable to have an unspoken thought.

As a simple practice, I sit quietly for 20 minutes twice a day (starting from two minutes a day ten years ago). I call this time "silence without a goal." Simply sit in silence (on your bed, at your work station, before an important meeting) and breathe slowly. This will have a remarkable, calming effect. This practice, however brief, is actually the heart of prayer. It is a time to just be still. When you first start this practice (and it does take practice), it is easy to get distracted and bored and restless. If I experience a distracting thought, I take a deep breath and become quiet again. There is no goal but to be quiet and still. While I don't "do silence" with any goal in mind, I have experienced a benefit. I can tell that I have learned to become calmer in tough situations when I used to become easily frustrated.

Another practice that I employ in moments of silence, such as in the car at a stoplight without the radio on, is something that my college philosophy professor, Dr. John Wickersham, called "the celebration of the senses." John taught us to call upon our senses of sight, smell, hearing, touch and taste to awaken us to the beauty around us.

In a quiet moment, recall:
• The sound of a young child's voice.
• The feel of the breeze or a light mist on your skin.
• The smell of bread baking.
• The sight of the sun setting.

These practices typically lead to a heightened sense of appreciation and calm. Patience is required. You are truly swimming against the cultural tide in this practice.

2. **Foster gratitude.** I went on a retreat at a monastery. While there, I visited with a monk who taught me what he called "The Gratitude Exercise."

This exercise is simple. You simply pause in silence several times a day and ask yourself two questions:
1. For what am I grateful in this moment?
2. What did I do to deserve this blessing?

I now do this exercise frequently in each day and I experience gratitude for many blessings:
- The meal in front of me.
- All of my senses work.
- The roof over my head.
- Conversations with my wife, sons or a friend.
- The companionship of our dog, Louie.

The monk who taught this exercise to me told me that the more I practiced gratitude, "the more grateful I would become for smaller and smaller things." This is absolutely the case.

- Walk through your school, hospital or agency. Look at the people in this place. If you are a church pastor, look at the people in the pews or in a meeting. Where is there a reason to be grateful?
- Walk around your home or look at the names in your phone directory. Where is there cause for gratitude?
- Awaken your senses. Where is there reason to be grateful?

> Look for thin places. Cultivate gratitude in a world that too often overlooks simple reasons to be grateful.

In Ireland, the ancient pagan Celts, and later the Christians, used the term *thin places* to describe the abiding beauty of the rocky coastline, offshore islands, the foliage and mountains. Heaven and earth appeared to meet when the sun rose and set over the sea. These are the thin places.

When we are jolted out of our old way of seeing things, when a conversation touches us and stays with us, when a student, patient or client experiences a breakthrough, we witness the thin places around us, the places where heaven and earth meet.

Look for thin places. Cultivate gratitude in a world that often overlooks reasons to be grateful.

3. **Foster your vital relationships.** Your relationship with your spouse, partner, children,

> These practices have helped me to experience the grace of God — to allow wisdom to break through where preoccupation, worry and doubt once ruled.

friends and mentors are windows to more thin places. These are the people who treasure you for who you are and not for your title or credentials.

The relationships are characterized by trust and intimacy. The word *intimate* comes from a root word in Latin which means "to enter your fear."

Our trusted companions, who arrive by way of family, friendship and collegiality, enable us to enter into our doubts, regrets, histories and fears and *redeem* them into opportunities for growth and the deepening of our spirit.

It is easy to neglect these relationships in favor of our professional commitments. What a shame to do so!

Tell these people how they matter to you. These are the people in your "trophy case." Trust them and encourage the same in them. I believe heaven meets earth in our loving relationships, pure and simple.

4. **Use these experiences of silence, gratitude and intimacy to equip you to serve and lead.**

In your role as a leader of a school, church, health or service community, you witness unforgettable levels of suffering and sorrow.

The previous three practices enable you to integrate these painful, difficult circumstances rather than avoid or resent them.

These practices have helped me to experience the grace of God and to allow wisdom to break through where preoccupation, worry and doubt once ruled.

FINAL THOUGHTS FOR BUSY, BUSY PEOPLE

Ready for one more airport story? Several years ago, I traveled to Oklahoma City for work. My return flight home was delayed by weather, so I headed for the food court to grab a soda and begin working on my laptop. Three soldiers were standing next to me and I overhead them planning to order a slice of pizza and a soda. I interrupted them and told them that I was eavesdropping. I asked if I could pay for their meals. They initially declined but I persisted. I assured them that I was at a point in life that this would not be a burden for me. One of the soldiers asked, "Are you sure?" I replied, "Absolutely. I'm happy to get this for your group."

The same soldier turned around to the **twenty-plus** solders whom I did not see assembled behind me and announced: "You guys! This guy is going to take care of our pizza!" (This is why my wife, Mary Ann, would encourage me to "not make eye contact" when I traveled.)

After Mr. Deep Pockets paid for their meals, I returned to a quiet area to catch up on my work. Several soldiers came to say thank you and one of them remarked: "You looked really shocked when you turned around." "I was, man," I replied. Several small conversations ensued while we waited for the weather to improve and enable us to resume our travels. One young man told me about joining the military out of a sense of duty but also to eventually complete his education. He told me that he lost his father when he was a senior in high school. In fact, his father collapsed and died at his football game. He told me how stunning and surreal it still felt. He wept as he told me of his grief, his dad's flaws and strengths and his concern for his mom.

What an encounter from an initial miscommunication. Then his flight was called and we had to part ways. We embraced and he said: "Thank you for being a father to me for a while today." What an honor.

Grace unfolds in moments like this. Be awake to such possibilities in your work community, in your love relationships and even in an airport food court.

Learn to tell time differently. I'm not talking about daylight savings time or time zones.

The Greeks had two words for time. One word was "chronos." It is the root word of chronological. Chronos was about the passage of time, segments of a day, or dates on a calendar. The other word for time was "kairos" which means "the opportune time," the time of transformation. We experience kairos when we lose ourselves in a conversation or when we experience a touching situation or when people's lives improve because of the efforts of our colleagues.

Learn to tell time in kairos.

Finally. Keep asking the airport questions of yourself and your organization. Doing so will equip you to cross many, many borders.

COURAGE:

To tell the STORY
of your life
with your
WHOLE
HEART.

■ CULTIVATING SPIRITUAL HEALTH

Donald Eggleston, M.Div., M.Ed.

The following is intended to serve as a quick reference for you.
Please use this to keep your focus during the extra-busy times.

CULTIVATE: **COURAGE***

- I have a job that reflects my soul
- I include my values and beliefs in my decisions
- I incorporate the well-being of others in my decision making
- I place the well-being of my family before my profession
- I make thoughtful decisions
- I foster growth in others
- I leave a legacy in each decision and interaction
- I am growing in faith and deepening in spirit

CULTIVATE: **AN INTERIOR LIFE**

- I know who I am
- I know what I value
- I live with a spirit of gratitude for the simple blessings in my life
- I set aside time for prayer and meditation
- I am more than my role, acquisitions or accomplishments
- I am consistently willing to learn
- I am reflective about my experiences and their meaning
- I am aware of my strengths and limitations and make important decisions with these in mind
- I integrate suffering and loss into my understanding of life

CULTIVATE: **COMMUNITY**

- I am in relationships where I am encouraged and challenged
- I share my gifts, talents, insights and vulnerability with others
- I am part of a church or a group that contributes to my growth in faith and hope
- I share credit for accomplishments
- I listen intently
- I have a love for the earth that is seen in my actions
- I willingly learn about people who are different from me

* "To tell the story of your life with your whole heart."

■ ABOUT THE AUTHOR

Donald Eggleston is the founder of Mission Works, LLC, a teaching and consulting resource in support of the achievement of organizational mission and purpose.

Don enjoyed a 30-year career in health care; serving in the areas of community outreach and organizational development, and concluded his career as vice president of Mission Integration for SSM Health in St. Louis, MO.

He has a Master of Divinity degree from Kenrick Seminary and a Master's Degree in Education from the University of Missouri — St. Louis.

Don also completed a certificate in Leadership of Organizational and Social Change from Case Western University.

He welcomes your thoughts and questions at Don@WithAllWeAreBook.com

Made in the USA
Lexington, KY
01 February 2018